Homeless Has A Name

Miriam Walker

Published by: Joseph's Ministry, LLC Consultant Group
www.josephsministryllc.com

DEDICATION

I would like to thank my mom and dad, for adopting me and setting me on this journey. Without you, I would not have found this path – and there would be no book.

And to the homeless men and women that are in these pages, the ones who shared their stories with me, the one's I will never see again, nor will I ever forget - I thank you.

This book is dedicated to you.

To my brother, may you have found your way home...

CONTENTS

PREFACE

Time is like a vapor. It is the one commodity we can never reproduce or get a refill on. There are no do-overs in life and despite our desire for more; once time is gone it is not coming back. It has been nearly six years since I last volunteered at the homeless shelter downtown, such long time ago. What began as a church outreach, turned into a 3-year stretch of meeting people, and listening to their stories, as I dished out goulash and tater tots.

Driving home I would think about what I had heard, and all that I'd seen. More often than not, the stories would form inside my mind, long before I had a chance to clean up, and sit down to my laptop.

I have always had a calling to tell a story, but not my own. Every homeless drifter has one, each one different from the last. Each story, with its beginning and ending, is filled with a life that had somehow began spinning in the wrong direction. The stories you are holding are all true – although the names and some defining characteristics, have been changed to protect the innocent. These forgotten drifters have existed unnoticed year after year. Each one has a story. Each one has a name.

Homeless Has A Name…

NOBODY CARES ABOUT AN ADDICT

I fell in love with stories long before I started writing them. Every time we come across another individual in our lives, it may be the last encounter. It may be very significant indeed. Something may happen during that exchange of time, in that moment - to change both of our lives forever.

It is in telling her story that I hope to present a narrative that would paint a very vivid picture of her life – at least the part of her life that she felt comfortable sharing with me, on this cold day outside the shelter. Brenda told me that more than anything she wanted to love herself; more than anything else in this world, that was what she wanted.

Brenda is addicted to cocaine, and she says she hates herself. They told her at rehab, that she had the strength on the inside of her to stop doing cocaine. She told me that even though they told her she had strength on the inside, she did not feel it. She felt only weakness. They told her to listen to the small voice inside that was telling her to stop; she told me she did not hear that voice.

Brenda's beginning was horrible, tainted and derailed with abuse, dysfunction and pain. She told me nobody ever told her it was not her fault; and so, she thought that it was. She shares that she is tired of rehab that it does not work for her. I immediately thought of all the families that stage interventions for their loved ones. Her family gave up on her years ago. I asked her if they knew where she was, or if she knew, where in fact, they were. She tells me that her family is not looking for her, and she is not sure where to start looking for them. "I'll just stay vanished," she says. There was nobody to stage an intervention for Brenda. And before me, I see a woman that is astoundingly good at faking what she feels. As she talks to me, I see a detachment, almost as if she is a spectator in her own life, and not the one living it. She is angry, but not at me. She seems distracted by my words, and unmoved by her own. However, beneath the anger where she is pretending she can't feel it, is pain. I see it in her sunken eyes. I can see it in the way she looks far off into the distance. I see it in the way she looks at me. As she talks, I listen to the story of a woman, who is a product of her own choices, and some choices, that were not her own. My heart breaks for Brenda as she sits before me, sharing with me bits and pieces of her life. I look into the sun-scorched face of this woman, that oddly looks out of place, on such a cold winter day, and I am saddened by her words.

Now it is much later.

As I sit in front of my laptop, and form my thoughts and memories into words, I recall what my friend Brenda told me before she left our meeting. She told me that nobody cared about a homeless addict, and because that is what she was, nobody cared about her. And as I fought to hold back tears, much the way I'm doing right now as I type, she walked away before I could tell her, that I did.

A VISIT WITH WALLACE

Friday night found me sitting next to an old friend. The dinner being held for the homeless was beginning, and I located an empty seat next to Wallace. I noticed him getting off the bus and then going in to find a seat. I met Wallace three years ago one Saturday night. Although he was living in the shelter at the time, with the other homeless people, he too was working in the kitchen with me. As we were preparing to leave for the evening, we gathered to pray. One of the others asked Wallace if he would like to join us and he said, very plainly, "Eff no." That began a two-year interaction with my friend Wallace.

Over time, he began to loosen and soften up a little. The angry demeanor began to fade, with me anyway. Wallace would still vent to the other homeless people and the security guards, and each interaction was filled with angry conversations loaded with profanity. One Saturday evening close to the holidays, I was next to Wallace on the serving line. Our conversation started about the weather, and then it turned to Thanksgiving. All of a sudden, and quite out of the blue, Wallace exclaimed, "I hate Thanksgiving. And I'm still mad at God." I asked Wallace why he hated the holiday. (I decided not to touch the hating God question – people have different reasons for stuff like that, and I figured that may or may not be a conversation for another day.)

Wallace told me that evening, while we were dishing out fish sticks and french fries, that two years ago, on Thanksgiving Day, his eight-year-old son died. His son had asthma, and on that day while in his mothers' care, he had a horrible asthma attack. To hear Wallace tell it, his son's mother was on drugs, and did not get him the help he needed. When he arrived home that day, his son was already gone. Wallace left the serving line at that point in the story. Without even realizing it, the shock of what Wallace had told me, stunned me into a slow-motion existence. The serving line very quickly backed up because of my lack of speed, not to mention Wallace had left the line. I glanced to where he had walked away, but he was gone.

Driving home after the dinner shift, I thought about my own son. I cannot even imagine what it would be like or feel like, to lose him. The evening was just beginning to overtake what was left of the sun, and as I drove, I thought about it. I thought about loss. I thought about the loss of a child. I thought about pain. And in that moment, driving down the expressway, I imagined that the pain would be so great, that I would end up hating everything surrounding when it happened, including the anniversary of the exact day it took place. Wallace hated Thanksgiving. I get it.

It would be weeks before I would see Wallace again. He unfortunately lost his spot in the kitchen, and eventually got kicked out of the shelter for being belligerent. When he did come in to get a food tray, he would always come find me and say hello.

This past Friday night was the first time I had seen Wallace in over a year. It made me happy to see my old friend. But I'll be honest, the happiness was practically overshadowed with the sadness I felt, for seeing him in the same place he was in a year ago; still homeless. I found my seat next to him and we caught up for a minute. Lost in my own private thoughts of time spent with Wallace in the kitchen of the shelter, the memories, once forgotten with the passing of time, are now coming very quickly. He was often angry, impulsive, quiet at times – but mostly angry. I glance over at one point, and I see tears running down Wallace's face.

I quickly turned away, as to not embarrass him. A few minutes pass, and I watch as my old friend walked out of the meeting, and into the hallway towards the kitchen.

Now as sit to write and allow my thoughts to become words on the page, I am faced with a realization that I already knew, but as chance would have it, I had to remind myself on Friday. Wanting something for someone, even wanting it badly for them, will not make it be. You can want it for them, but you cannot make them want it. Everyone has a choice. Everyone has the ability to hope – but sadly, some must look a little bit harder to find it. Sometimes hope is hidden very deeply, behind all the pain and the tragedy. However, hope is there, in the tiny seeds sown, by the people that care.

My friend Wallace was not a homeless drifter before his son died. He was not unemployed, and by his own admission, he was not an angry man. And as I think back to

Friday night, watching the tears slowly falling down his face, I suspect that he might not be mad at God any longer – can't say for sure of course, but the tears may point to something other than anger. One can only hope...

HIS NAME IS LESTER

"The fact is - that five years ago I was, as near as possible, a different person to who I am tonight. I, as I am now, didn't exist at all. Will the same thing happen in the next five years? I hope so."

- Siegfried Sassoon

IF THIS NOTE GOES UNREAD, THAT WOULD BE OK. If nothing else, it will serve as a reminder to me, if to no one else, of the ongoing problem that we have in our city, in our community, in our own backyard. A day will come, and I will open this story... and read it to remind MYSELF, that although there has been progress and triumphs, there is more work that needs to be done, than has been done. In a perfect world I suppose, one could make a request for help and the help will come. Other times it takes more than a request, something else is needed. Occasionally change is needed. Every so often, it takes a story - it takes an account of the blunt, abrupt, chronicle of events, unfolding right before your very eyes.

The reader is not privy to the explicit details, and so it is left up to the writer to illustrate and to interpret; to reproduce if you will, making sure not to leave out any subtle details, as to what is really happening before you. In short, truth. Pure unadulterated truth. The gentleman at the center of this story is homeless.

His name is Lester. A year ago, Lester approached me on a Saturday evening, and told me I needed to wash my truck. He was right, it needed a good washing. That comment started a series of back and forth banter that I came to enjoy, whenever I would go to the shelter. Lester looked to be fifty-something, later fifties I would guess. He is a homeless man, and he stays at the shelter. I learned early on, that Lester had a couple of kids living in Muskogee. He would always ask me about my kids; how the oldest was doing, how the girls were doing, and most recently, how my grandson was doing. One day I asked him about his children. And as an over tanned hand, darkened and weathered from the sun, pulled out the photo from a tattered falling apart wallet, I noticed a smile on his face, as he shared his family with me. Lester is a good guy. We talk football over the serving line, as we occasionally hold up the serving line. He teases me about my team and I make fun of his.

Each evening when I sign out to leave, Lester would wait at the door, ready to make sure I got to my truck safely. As the summer gives way to autumn, and then the winter months overtake us, it would get darker much earlier. Many times, it would already be dark when I would leave. Lester tells me, "Miriam, you need to park over there," and he points to an area of the lot that had a light pole. "That way you're right under the camera." Good old Lester. After I changed my parking spot to accommodate the security camera and the lights, he was still there every evening, making sure I got into my truck. I had known him for more than two years, when I began to notice that he was not coming in as much anymore. I asked the kitchen boss, "Where's Lester?" He only shrugs, does not know.

This past Saturday to my surprise, in walks my friend. I was not only shocked to see him; I was completely and utterly unprepared for what I saw. It was almost as if my eyes were playing a dirty trick on my mind, or vice versa. TIME. Time is an unforgiving foe. This was not the Lester that came through the line over the past two years. This man came in without a smile. A set of very shaky weathered hands reached out and took the tray set before him. He might have recognized me, perhaps not. He went to sit down. Therefore, it was with some apprehension and inner sadness that I went over to see about my friend. "Lester, what's up?" He makes eye contact. "Miriam," he says, "How are them girls?" He was shaking as he sat.

It is common knowledge among the volunteers that frequently work at the shelter, that there is a large number of mentally ill, physically impaired, and seriously addicted people living under that roof. Although I cannot speak on what was causing Lester to shake, my mind went many places. I go back to help with the cleanup with a heavy heart. As Lester walks out, he does not look towards the serving line as he usually did - he very slowly walks out of the kitchen and into the evening air. My friend Lester seems to have forgotten how to hope. As I had predicted in my mind's eye, he was not waiting for me when I got finished that night.

There are moments that stay frozen in time. It comes as no surprise, to me anyway, that this past Saturday evening was one of those moments. It was clear to me, in seeing my old friend, that time, or perhaps drugs, or both, seems to have wiped his expectations away. There are homeless shelters full of amazing people that have just forgotten how to hope. My friend Lester is just one of many.

I CAN'T FIND IT

When the boy came through the line, he came through like everyone else, or so it seemed. It was well within the realm of possibility, that he was just like all the other homeless people coming to eat supper. However, sometimes there are things that we do not see coming – accidents, we do not always see those coming. Unexpected falls; we do not see those coming either. A teenager, so drugged out and inebriated on God knows what, walking through the line at the homeless shelter; I did not see that coming, nor did I expect it. What I found saddest of all was that he could not have possibly been more than 15 years old. I ask him for his bed ticket, as I was in the front of the serving line. Because I had an established worker breathing down my neck, I asked him a second time, and then I quickly said "thank-you" so he would just take a tray and go sit down. (I would go and get his bed ticket.)

He did not sit down; instead, he looked up. When his eyes met mine, it was as if he was looking right through me, but he was not focused on me. His eyes were glassy, and he was swaying towards the front of the serving line and I asked him again, if he checked in. He could have stayed anyway, but he needed a ticket to get a cot after supper, and so I asked him if he could go get his ticket, so that he could get his bed.

He speaks. "What?" He gets a confused look on his face. "Can you check in, so you'll have a bed for later? You need a ticket." He asks me, "Is this the shelter? I thought this was the homeless shelter." "It is," I tell him, "do you want to eat? Get a ticket and come back through the line and you can eat. You need a ticket, so they'll save you a bed for later." And I watch his face. He is not talking, but I am listening. I am listening for any sound at all, that could make sense of any of this. He says, "Where is this? Am I at the shelter?"

About this time, the lady behind me escorts him to get a ticket. I tell her to make sure he checks in, so he will have a bed. She comes back and as it turns out, they ask him his name to see if he was already in the system, that way they could just check him in. She says every time they ask him for his name, he just says, "I can't find it." Then he leaves. As I drive home from the shelter, I find myself thinking about this boy. He was not a man. He might have been a teenager, but just barely. Things that affect you more deeply are remembered with greater clarity, which is why I have been seeing his face off and on since that night. It was a very sad situation. When I left the shelter that night, I looked all around to see if I could see the boy. I honestly do not know what I would have done had I seen him but it does not matter now – that was the last time I ever saw him.

IT'S ONLY TEMPORARY

The following is a true story. There are no names to change, as she never shared with me, what her name was. Thinking back now, some 3 weeks later from our last meeting, I find myself wondering why she did not tell me her name. Therefore, there is nothing in the following account that needs to be masked or concealed. The young lady in the center of this story, had a childhood lost, entirely due to the choices of another. I wondered to myself, how many others had no choice. I met her one evening before the dinner shift was getting ready to begin.

This chance encounter, which played out at the homeless shelter, was rare indeed. It is not often, that I am afforded the time to sit and visit with the people that frequent the shelter. This is her story, as told to me, over the course of several meetings. I am not talking; I am only listening...

My slowly clearing mind begins to reflect. I remember being left alone, being pulled out of schools, an abrupt slap when entering a room when I should not have - all these memories shaped my adolescent years. The earliest memories are the worst, as they are more vivid, and not clouded by the numbing haze that comes from too much alcohol, or one too many hits. Over time, the numbing became a necessity. Time passes as it always will - and now as I stand in front of the clipboard at the shelter, a shaking hand has a hard time steadying the pen. So many blanks to fill in. I know my address, or lack thereof. Homeless. It is what brought me here.

I know who I am, I just don't know who I've become. As I became a teenager, there were so many errors in judgment - miscalculated decisions. Every day was a series of choices; turns to right when I should have gone left. As I became older, I began to forget what it was like to be me, before everything turned horrible. But far earlier than my teenage years, as a young girl, I learned very quickly, that if I snuck out to the late night parties my mother would hold, I could follow behind and finish off half empty glasses, of whatever the party goer left behind. There were so many parties, and so I came to welcome the sensation that would follow. It seemed to make the slaps coming from my mother less painful; the being left alone was not nearly as lonely.

Although I enjoyed the feelings that came from the liquid in the forgotten glasses, there was always the fear that one of my mother's invited friends would come see about the forgotten child in the back room. That I, a young child became quickly drunk, from sneaking leftovers from a party, was an unfortunate reality. However, it did make the horrifying events in the back seem a little less horrifying.

As I grew older, I grew smarter. There were things I learned to avoid. I became skilled in the art of sneaking and running. I realized that with perfect timing, I could get the drinks, which I had grown to crave, and then hit the road. The unwanted abusive advances from my mother's male friends ended, but not until I was shaped into a very damaged young lady, emotionally and physically. They ended for good the weekend I turned ten. I gathered all my strength and decided to tell the secret. By the time I entered my first foster care home, my body had already been conditioned to need the alcohol, and my mind became programmed on how to get it, at whatever the cost. That did not fare well for most of the homes in which I lived. The ongoing battle of me needing the alcohol, and the foster parent not willing to provide what I needed, ultimately became too much to handle. Therefore, I ran, again and again.

As a young girl, I saw, I learned, and I did. My introduction into a lifestyle of alcoholism began before I even realized it. The life I had begun to live was shaped out for me, and it was in fact, what ultimately brought me to this place. Homelessness. As my shaking hand failed miserably at filling out the form in front of me, I felt someone touch my arm. I did not look up to see who it was, but I heard the words, "It's only temporary." Temporary. I could handle that. I was tired, so tired. I was ready for new memories, happy memories. The mental snapshots that I had been carrying for nearly a decade, were wearing me down. Although I was as much frightened as I was nervous, walking into the shelter, I felt a small seed of hope. That seed took root as I heard the words of the stranger. Temporary. I was done with the running, and I was ready to make a change.

Now it is much later.

In the story, I was the stranger that touched her arm, and told her it was only temporary. I am not sure what became of my friend after all those meetings at the shelter. I began to see her less and less, and soon she stopped coming through the dinner line altogether. As I sit now, drawing on the memories of those talks with my friend, the one who would not tell me her name, I close my eyes and try to picture her face.

It is only temporary...

NO, I DON'T WANT YOUR DUMB MAGAZINES

There is this lady that comes through the dinner line every Saturday night. Mean as a snake. She never smiles when I speak to her, but instead rolls her eyes. (Sure, she was homeless and probably did not have much to smile about, but she was downright nasty to us, while we served her.) One night we brought her some magazines. The ladies liked to keep those for reading, so one of us would stop by the thrift store or Walmart, and pick up a few. She threw them in the trash right in front of us! (That was almost funny, as it was so blatantly "take this and shove it!)

One Saturday night as chance would have it, I was cleaning up around her table, and she was looking at a few photos. I asked to see them, FULLY expecting to be PUNCHED in the throat! However, she did not punch me - instead she started talking. She showed me a photo of two boys, her sons. They looked to be about 15 or so. She tells me she had two, and they both died, both OD'ing on drugs many years ago. All I could think to say was... nothing. No words would have been adequate. I was speechless. She kept talking, but my mind had already left the conversation. I was in shock, and now it all made sense. I checked back into the conversation as I continued to clean, then she got up and left.

A couple of weeks later we tried again. We brought her some magazines and a couple of paperbacks. She waited until she knew we were watching, she looked in the kitchen where we stood, watching, and then she threw them in the trash. You will never as long as you live, meet somebody that is not going through something. Some things are very small, while others leave you wondering, how they are even making it through each new hour in their day...

Miriam Walker

ROBERT'S STORY

Robert's hand shook nervously to light his second cigarette, although it might have been his third. I quickly lost count, as he flicked the smoldering butts into the air. They landed hard, skipping once or twice along the pavement. This was a different meeting for us. Usually we talked over the serving line, me serving the vegetables, him handing out the bread and milk for the kids. Today we were outdoors, on the bench in front of the shelter. It appears Robert wanted to talk, and so I let him and as he talked, I listened. And right there on that bench outside the shelter, my friend Robert shared a story that will remain with me forever.

I had the good fortune of meeting Robert a couple years back, as he was going through a program at the homeless shelter that offered him help in finding his own permanent housing. In exchange for that help, Robert went to job placement classes, and was required to help in the kitchen. The conversations took off from there. As we served the people coming through, the adrift and the displaced of our city, we talked; rather he talked. Mostly I just listened.

Robert is an alcoholic and he has been homeless, by his own admission, for more than eight years. Sometimes you can lose everything, and still no lasting change occurs. That was the case with Robert. It was his drinking that caused him to lose his family, his home, and ultimately caused him to lose his place in the shelter program. I smelled alcohol on him as he spoke to me that day outside the shelter. Although he was not intoxicated, it could not have been too long before this meeting that he was. Alcohol and cigarette smoke hung stale in the air. Now as I sit down to write, and allow my thoughts to become words, it is that smell that is etched in my memory – and the words that he spoke to me that afternoon, are etched in my mind. This is his story.

The day Robert's brother died he was the only one in the house, babysitting. He was 12, not yet a teenager, but it was easy on most days. His mom always left complete instructions- when to feed, when to check diapers, no friends over and always leave the baby in the crib or the playpen. Robert liked that rule the best, leaving him free to play his video games. He was 12 after all. On this day, the video playing was intense because he had a friend over. Giving little or no thought to the "no friends over" rule, the battle between the two boys waged on for hours in front of the TV set. Robert's friend left for dinner and he played a little bit longer before checking on his brother. By the time he finally made it to the baby's room, his brother was dead. Robert's brother died of SIDS that day, sudden infant death syndrome.

The next few years were a blur, clouded by sadness, remorse and guilt. His mother began to treat him with indifference, going so far as to let days go by without speaking to him. He knew she blamed him for his brother's death; he blamed himself as well. Robert shares with me, that his mother never told him it was his fault- but she never told him it was not. As Robert pauses to light another cigarette, I can see his sad eyes looking into the distance. I noticed of the two of us that I was the one crying. I guess it made sense. He had been living this story his whole life. It was all new to me. New and sad.

He shifts slightly on the bench outside the shelter and begins again. Robert says the drug use started in Jr. High when he was fifteen. After realizing it was easier to get booze, he started drinking that, claiming that the alcohol helped him to forget. It helped him escape the memory of his brother lying still and unmoving in his crib. He sees the picture in his mind every day, and so he drinks every day, to forget. He often wondered why it was so easy to drink around his mother. She never said anything, never stopped him, and never even mentioned it. It was years before he realized why. She too was drinking to forget. Robert's familiarity with life's reservoir of cruelties began very early indeed. There is not a day that goes by that he does not feel guilt and sadness, guilt for having a friend over, guilt for not checking on the baby sooner, and the sadness that can only come from the unfeeling detachment of a mother. Every day he faced the mental snapshots that he didn't know how to shake, and so he continues to escape the only way he knew how, with alcohol.

Leaving home at the age of 18, he tried his hand at many jobs, but they never lasted. He would show up to work drunk, he drank on the job, and if they could not tell he had been drinking, his overall performance lacked what it took to remain gainfully employed. He lost job after job. My friend Robert stops talking long enough, to flick another cigarette butt into the air. I quickly became focused on watching it smolder on the hard asphalt. I watched as the smoke continued to circle into the stale air. (It is strange the things our mind selects to remember – the details we choose to carry as memories; what stays, and what disappears from our mind. I cannot recall the number of children Robert said that he had but only that he had them. However, I do remember how long it took that cigarette to smolder out on the pavement, exactly one minute.)

Robert stands to fish a lighter out of his pocket and drops it on my shoe. As he bends to pick it up, I notice his weathered hand beginning to shake. He hurries to pick it up, embarrassed that I had noticed. He lights another cigarette and continues with his story. He was married on two different occasions. His first marriage ended just in time.

(Those were his words.) Both he and his wife were alcoholics; both were young, and neither ready to settle down. The two fought endlessly, the worst fight ending with her leaving. She never came back. Robert had children with his second wife. He tells me that he was drunk so often, that all his memories seemed false, not real, clouded by a drunken haze that never ended. He was in fact drunk in the hospital when his wife gave birth to his child. I watch as his eyes begin to mist over and the tears fall.

When Robert saw his newborn for the first time, he cried right there in the hallway in front of the nursery window, much like he was crying in front of me now. He pauses for what seems like several minutes and then begins again. "It wasn't my child I saw in the crib that day, it was my brother." He left his second wife and child that day in the hospital. This time he was the one that never went back. He continues to pause as he is talking, as if he is waiting for me to respond. My mind was filled with the things I could say, but I am not talking, I am simply listening. Although there were thoughts that screamed out in my head, I did not let them turn into words. I kept them silent.

Robert left Iowa for good, thinking that maybe the distance from his past would take away the horrible memories. He ended up in Tulsa a broken man, but a man determined to stop the drinking once and for all. Getting into the shelter was tougher than he had imagined. The security guards were already familiar with his drinking, as if they knew he was coming and knew what to expect. Robert quickly realized that they were not singling him out, but anyone who was drinking. This gave him a small seed of hope. He did need a place to sleep after all. He very quickly signed up for a program that would allow him to stay at the shelter, help him to find employment, and eventually help him get his own apartment. Things were looking up for Robert.

Robert's addiction to alcohol was stronger than his desire for change. He wanted to change, and by his own admission, he tried repeatedly. Many times, working with him in the kitchen, I could tell he had been drinking. Although he was not staggering or slurring his words, the smell was unmistakable. I was one of many that did not make a big deal about it. He would tell me bits and pieces of his life even though I never asked. It was as if he HAD to tell somebody. As I write now, I recall, nearly two years later, the pain was there. I could see his pain clearly enough, as clearly as I can feel my sadness for him, even now. Robert began missing the Saturday dinner shift and very soon, I saw him less and less. More often than not, he was prevented from coming in due to his drunken state at the time. It was on one such Saturday that I saw him on the bench outside the shelter as I was parking. He waves, and I go tell him hello. His sun scorched face managed a smile as he puffed away on a cigarette. "Robert," I ask him, "Where have you been friend?" As a shaking hand tries to steady the cigarette to his lips, Robert fills me in on how he has been. As he talks, the alcohol and the smoke remain stagnant in the air surrounding me. My mind drifts and I imagine that five minutes ago, I was still driving to the shelter, and not sitting on the bench with Robert. He talked, and I listened.

I never saw Robert again after our meeting in front of the shelter. As earlier stated, he did in fact lose his placement in the program. It really was a chance encounter me even seeing him that day. I call it divine appointment. It is hard to tell where he ended up. The kitchen manager seems to think he may have gone back to Iowa. However, I sometimes think I see him walking along the street. He looks a lot like the other homeless men I see aimlessly wandering about. I suppose it could be Robert. I think about him often and wonder how he is getting along. The heart re-visits memories often, without prior notice that that is where the heart is going. And every time I think about my friend

Robert, my heart is saddened, for the life that had begun spinning in the wrong direction. I hope to see him again one day...

Miriam Walker

DON'T MIND ME

Tuesday's trail finds me without my water. I was riding my bike yesterday, and I forgot it. And so, as I neared one of the water fountains that are stationed along the trail, I saw this lady, and she appeared to be washing up in the giant fountain, that was located by the small water fountain. She was dressed, but she was kind of wringing out a wet shirt, and there was an extra shirt, also wet, laying over a bench, and she was wet. She looked to be about 50 or so and had two large backpacks on the bench next to the wet shirt. I assumed she was homeless. I kind of inched up very slowly as to not startle her, and as I did, I looked all over. I did not

see anyone with her, nor did I see a bike. Definitely homeless
- maybe not. (That is odd. I have passed that fountain
probably 100 times before and have never seen anything
like that.) I see her, she sees me, and if I were not so thirsty,
I would have turned around. She instantly turned red with
embarrassment.

She began apologizing and stammering a little bit, and
of all the things that went through my head in that split-
second moment - the main thought that took over all the
others, was please, don't apologize. I tell her do not worry
about it and I get some water. I keep riding.

Of course, my thoughts stayed on that lady the whole
ride. I wonder what brought her to that point in her life,
homeless and washing in a public fountain. I wonder if she
had kids and if they knew where she was. I do not know. To
me, it was more sad than shocking. I realize the sight of a
lady washing up in a public fountain would shock some

people, possibly make them angry. It only really made me sad. Now as I sit, home from my ride, I am going through my photos and I find my mind returning to that brief encounter at the fountain. I wonder where she is now, and I wonder what all she has lost in the past 10 years. And if something is lost, would it ever be found again?

In every life there is a story, and the story tells you everything you need to know. I don't know anything about the lady at the fountain, and I don't know her story.

What I do know, is that she matters.

And I wonder if she knows it...

Miriam Walker

YOU GOT ANY CIGARETTES?

Saturday morning finds my daughters and me running some errands. We stop at McDonald's for a later than usual breakfast. I thought it was odd, that the two men sitting towards the back of the restaurant were drinking openly from a tall bottle of something, still in the bag; it was still so early. That is not something you see every day. I got my girls settled at a table, and I approach the men, and asked if they had eaten. They look at me at the same time, and one of them said, "I had a coffee." Then the one nursing the bottle said, "YOU GOT ANY CIGARETTES?" I began to laugh and told him, "Uhh, no. No, I do not. I do not have any cigarettes. Do you want a burger?" So he begins to laugh, that I had laughed at him, and I left to get them some hamburgers.

I had no idea what their story was. I could tell by the bags and belongings on the floor by their table, that they were more than likely homeless. I had no idea why they were drinking alcohol so early in the morning, and at a family restaurant. And as I think back now, a few days removed from when this happened, I recall, that I really didn't know much about these two strangers in the McDonalds that morning – I just know that it looked like they really needed some lunch.

I could have judged them I suppose, but in all honesty, it was only ten in the morning, and they were drinking out in the open in a family restaurant. There is a strong chance, that they had probably been judged enough for one day. As my daughters and I finish our brunch, I notice the men getting up to leave. A few minutes later, we did the same, and wouldn't you know it, those two men are sitting on the curb right in front of my vehicle. I give them a little wave, and one of them says, "Hey thanks for the burgers... you got any cigarettes?" No. No, I do not.

Miriam Walker

STUCK IN REVERSE – SYDNEY'S STORY

I met Sydney three years ago. This 6' 4" tall giant of a man visited the projects one Sunday afternoon, while we were doing a homeless outreach. The rapport he built with all of us was strong, and after that first visit, he was there every time we were.

Sydney told me he used to play basketball overseas, and judging from the looks of him, I believed it. He was good-natured, talkative, and he never met a stranger. Sydney is stuck in reverse.

I found out that at the time, his home was the projects. Even though there were many homeless people meandering about, he was not one of them. Many days he would make his way to the outreach smelling of marijuana. From time to time, it seemed, judging from his behavior, something much stronger held him bound. Regardless, we visited with him, joked around, and did our best to love him beyond his circumstances, beyond his choices.

As time went on, we switched to a different location in the city, and we did not see Sydney anymore after that. I often wondered what became of the very tall man that hung out with us on Sunday afternoons.

By a very chance encounter, I saw Sydney again one Saturday night at the shelter. We recognized each other right away. He asked whatever happened to us, and why we stopped giving out pizza by the projects way back then. I filled him in and asked what he had been up to lately.

Sydney tells me, as he danced back and forth from one foot to the other, that awhile back he "caught" a drug charge and went to jail. As a result, he lost his apartment in the projects and is now homeless. Then he asked me what they were serving in the kitchen, but he rushed off before I could answer.

He had not changed much my friend Sydney – he had the same hyper and jittery mannerisms that he had three year earlier. I know very little of what Sydney's life has been up to this point. I do not know when he became addicted. I do not know the path that led this man to homelessness. Was it one defining choice, or a series of choices that have significantly affected his life? No way to tell really. There is always something more to know in a life – and it is often what we do not know, that defines current situations.

Hope is often lost among the endless hard times that one encounters. Then sometimes, hope is found. It seems that every time I see Sydney, despite the places he continues to find himself in, I always see hope in his eyes. Soon he filters in behind the rest of the homeless men. As he takes his tray, he gives me a quick upward head nod. Then he is gone.

Miriam Walker

THE CUBBY

I sat down at the table next to the small girl with the brown hair. As soon as she notices me, she smiles, showing her missing front teeth. "You lost your two front teeth, didn't you?" She shakes her head yes and continues to smile her toothless grin. She had cornbread by her mouth. Her smile quickly fades, and she gets a serious look on her face. She asks me, "Did you know I had two shirts on?" I tell her, "No. I didn't know that." She continues. "Mom told me to wear them both, so they won't get stolen out of our box." "Oh really?" "Yes," she says. "It's kind of like a cubby but not like the one I had in the first grade. It's really a box under our cot but I pretend it's our cubby."

I smile at her and her ability to imagine and make believe, while surrounded by unimaginable circumstances, some of which she may not even be aware. She smiles back and asks me, "Do you know who my mom is?" She points, "She's right over there." I turn to follow her pointing finger, and I see her mom arguing with a man. It looks like an intense argument and so I distract the girl with a question. "What grade are you in?" She tells me she used to be in the first grade before they moved, but now she is not in school anymore. "I don't miss my teacher from the first grade because she wasn't nice. I only miss hot lunch and my cubby."

I smile at her and give a little laugh. She asks me why I was laughing. I tell her, "I think it's cool that you liked your cubby so much. What color was it?" "It was see through," she says, "but I found some Hello Kitty stickers and decorated it. Brandon tried to take the stickers off, but I caught him and stomped on his foot." Then she quickly stood and stomped on an imaginary foot.

I notice her mom still arguing, and so I drag out the cubby conversation. "Who's Brandon?" She gets a fierce look on her face and says, "He's not nice and he tried to ruin my cubby. But even though I had to stomp on his foot, now I miss him. And I miss my cubby too."

She all of a sudden hops up from the table and turns to leave. She gives me a little wave, and then she was gone. Just like that. I get up and begin to clean the cornbread crumbs from the table. I turned to look to see where she ran, and as I did, I found myself wishing I had some stickers for her... for her cubby under the cot.

Miriam Walker

ON TOP OF THE GRASS

I MET THIS MAN ONCE – I was at the time, working at the shelter during the dinner rush, and he came in with a group of men off the street. As was my normal greeting, I ask him, "How you doin' sir?" He looks at me and smiles; showing the very few teeth he had left in his mouth. His sun scorched face immediately lights up and he exclaims, "I'm doin' good!" Then he points upward towards the ceiling and continues, "Any day I wake up on TOP of the grass is a good day!" He gives me this happy wink of his eye, and proceeds to take his tray and move along down the line. As I continue to dish out beefy macaroni, his words resonated and touch my heart.

Here he is without a home, wearing at least three layers on a very hot afternoon, toting a faded knapsack no doubt containing all that is left of his worldly possessions –

And he is happy to be waking up on top of the grass. Alive!!

THE MAN, THE BABY, AND THE VISITOR

He was never defined by his addiction. Although he admitted to having one, he refused to believe that it affected his behavior. To hear him tell it, when it mattered the most, he could hold it together. If the truth were told, when it did matter the most, he did hold it together.

The baby came all of a sudden. They knew he was coming; they just did not know he would be so close to home, in their home. They were unprepared for the baby's arrival. The habits had no chance to fizzle out. The addictions had no time for deliverance.

The man took the lead. He had no experience with babies, and to care for one as tiny and as beautiful as this one, left him feeling highly inadequate; but he did it. The baby boy soon began to count on the man for his bath, for his bottle, for his attention.

The addiction was strong, stronger than the man realized. Although he took very good care of the baby, soon the baby had to leave. This made the man very sad. He thought that he was handling everything pretty well. Having let his habit take the lead role in his life, he soon loses touch with rational decisions. The home where he took care of the young baby boy ceases to be his home. He drifts through life – and becomes homeless.

Many years later, while sitting at a table with countless other homeless men and women, the unexpected visitor shows the man pictures of the baby boy. By some twist of fate, they have intertwined once again. The baby has grown and is now a toddler. The man smiles as he remembers the baby's grin, his bright eyes, his beautiful face, and his curly black hair. He asks the visitor if God hears all prayers. The visitor, holding back tears of gratitude and sadness combined answers "Yes. God hears every prayer." The man smiles as he lights a cigarette. He is happy on this night. He sees that all the love that he poured out on the baby boy was not wasted. He could tell by the photos that he was still very happy. The visitor smiles while driving away. She too - is happy on this night.

Miriam Walker

THE TENT UNDER THE BRIDGE

I met a guy this weekend. We will call him Raymond. It really was just a chance encounter; same place at the same time sort of thing. He had just recently bought a house in the area, and we were discussing fair market value and the neighborhood.

The conversation went on from there, and he shared with me that he had worked with a couple different companies in the city, different outreaches and such. He seemed like a nice guy. Then he tells me that he used to live in a tent. "Really?" I ask him, "A tent?" "Yep. A tent. Well, I use to live in a house with my family. I had a wife and three kids, but that was a very long time ago." Then Raymond gets this faraway look in his eyes, and he just stops talking.

It is quiet for a while, and I change the subject to pizza. Then Raymond changes it back to the tents. He goes on to share, that for a long time he lived under the bridges of San Francisco in a tent. He was homeless for many years. I smile at him – he gets a confused look on his face. I tell Raymond that I think that is amazing. "What?" he says, "That I lived in a tent?" I respond, "No, that you recently bought your own home. That's what's amazing."

I love it when I meet people I would not ordinarily meet, and I was happy to meet him that day. My friend Raymond answers the proverbial questions: Can people move on to happiness, from tragedy? Can you totally turn your life around, once your life has ended up in disarray and homelessness? Raymond shows us you absolutely can.

There are times when what is supposed to happen, does not actually happen. There is a detour of some sort - an unexpected event or an unforeseen episode, which causes your world to spin in the wrong direction. That is what happened to Raymond. Although I know only a fraction of his story, the part that I do know – has him standing with me on that hot summer day, handing out pizza slices to the homeless.

Our stories do not always turn out how we would have written them. Raymond shared very little of what caused him to end up in a tent, under the bridges of San Francisco. And I still do not know to this day. No. Not every story gets its happy ending. However, Raymond's did.

Miriam Walker

WHAT'S YOUR HURRY?

Friday morning finds me rushing through the store, on a mission for diapers and coffee. Because it was an all of a sudden and disappointing discovery, made very early after I woke up, I was kind of in a hurry. As I am walking very quickly down the isles I needed to be on, completely out of the blue, a gentleman steps out in front of me, walking very slowly. Very very slowly.

He had on a faded backpack jammed to the brim, and was holding several tattered plastic bags, as he slowly made his way through the store. His sneakers were very faded and covered in dry dirt. They were also nearly covered by his pants, which were a bit too long for him.

I could tell by the way he looked, and possibly, by the way he smelled, that he perhaps was homeless. I cannot say for sure of course, and I did not ask him. I suppose he could have lived somewhere. Judging from the near spilling contents from his tattered bags – one is left to wonder what was really going on. He slowly walked, as if he was numbly going through the motions of one foot in front of the other.

At that point, I just slowed down. I decided that I was not in that big of a hurry that I needed to rush past him, so I just fell into step behind him and slowed my pace. However, by then it was too late. He noticed me behind him and so he stepped aside and let me go past.

When he saw me behind him, he looked me in the eyes for just a moment. I said good morning very quickly and continued past. He seemed confused, almost lost in the grocery store. Yes – he looked lost. I quickly pay for Bub's diapers and my coffee and leave the store.

As I stopped in the parking lot waiting to drive onto the street, I noticed that same man standing in the metro area transit bus shelter. He was not facing the street; he was facing the store – which was how I noticed that he was crying. He had set his belongings down on the bench, and he was wiping his now reddened face; crying.

As I drove home, I could not help but wonder why he was so sad. The sight of this grown man crying made me sad but I wonder now, after the fact – why I did not notice his sadness in the store. I noticed his faded backpack, I noticed his tattered bags, he had three of them. I noticed his slow-paced walking as well as the time, as I was running late.

I noticed the smell, and I noticed the faded dirty sneakers. I noticed that his pants were too long, and that the contents of the bags he was carrying, were close to spilling out onto the clean grocery store floor. But I didn't notice his sadness. I could see that he looked lost, maybe confused as to what he was buying in this store. I could see that he was almost moving in slow motion through life but I did not see his sadness.

Had I sensed it in the store, would it have made a difference – would I have made a difference? Had I noticed in the store, that he was at the tipping point and ready to cry, would it have mattered? Would I have slowed down long enough to care?

That is the funny thing about regret. We can look back and imagine doing something totally different. We can revisit those places that we find ourselves in and wonder what could have been done differently. Life offers no do-overs. The first time around often comes with the finality of the choices we have decided to make. I saw a man in the metro transit bus shelter this morning. And although he was sad enough to start crying – I have no idea why, because I did not see it when I had the chance.

WILL THERE BE AN INTERVENTION?

The streets are thick with stories, ready to be discovered. Everywhere you turn is a plot, just waiting to be unfolded; like the pen of a ready writer...

I have a favorite show. There are a few that I watch on a normal basis, but my favorite by far has always been "Intervention" on the A & E Channel. Addiction - displayed in all its tormenting personality for the world to see. In the end of each episode, they play the signature music and begin to share "the update" if you will: "So and so has flourished, gone on to sober living, and has been sober since 2012..."Or dreadfully, "So and so left the program and moved back to the city..." Addiction and the final update - bookends to a life consumed by drugs or alcohol. The final update is the needed end of the episode, and I will watch until the end every time. I like to discover if somebody overcame the demons that had taken over their world.

THE ONE THING that all these people have in common, every single one, is that they all had somebody, often many people that cared. They have loved ones that called the show and said, "Hey! I cannot handle this! Please help me!" Regardless of the outcomes, these addicts were loved in such a way, that their family members went on national television and exposed the worst part of their lives. Addiction is the worst part of a life. The stories continue, often without a happy ending.

I was thinking about this show this afternoon, as I drove to the shelter for the dinner shift. It was on that drive, that an article about the chronic homelessness crisis in America came to mind. I was reminded of a time while serving one evening, and then another time, and then another evening after that, and night after night, they would come through the line, often shaking as they balanced their food tray. The sun-scorched hands, unsteady from the withdrawal symptoms, often shook violently as they reached for their dinner. An addict that does not get their "fix" will often shake uncontrollably and sadly, this is the memory that rises to the top each evening.

Unfortunately, there is no rehab for the homeless addict. There will be no drug intervention show for a man or woman that has lost touch and lost family, on their unfortunate journey to this bleak new reality. It is not that nobody cares about a homeless addict because many do care. Many churches and many individuals volunteering care very much, but it is a problem far bigger than one person or one church.

Many addicts will stay homeless because they cannot afford rehab. They cannot or do not work, because they are addicted. They cannot pay rent because they cannot work - because an addict will never keep a job for long. The cycle continues, and the shelter becomes their home.

We often judge the homeless addict laying under a bridge next to a tattered backpack. And sure, they might just take the few dollars made on the highway and go buy a half pint of liquor, just enough to keep the shakes at bay. It's what an addict does, it's a sad reality. Many of the homeless used to have loved ones, and many still do, they just don't know where they have ended up.

I see Jamal nearly 3 times a month during the dinner shift. He is a 40-year-old man from Ohio, by way of Muskogee, living in the Tulsa shelter. He looks like he is 70 years old. Jamal told me he has many kids, and when I asked him where his kids were, he said he thinks his family was in

Ohio. While speaking, he shakes so badly that we take turns carrying his tray to his table as he carries a sad disposition on his face that silently says, "It's no use."

The stories from the streets will always be there. The homeless addict will more than likely always be there and there will always be people who care. But it's a cycle – it's like an hourglass that has been nailed to the table. Time stops unless and until somebody turns it over. The need for the show intervention will always be there, but divine intervention is what is needed most - especially for the homeless addict.

Miriam Walker

FLAMIN' HOT FUNYUNS

I saw Debra the first time as I rode by; and it was then that I knew I would be stopping on my way back. The stale heat that was engulfing me as I rode my bike, made the opportunity to stop and take a break very appealing. However, I doubt her name is Debra.

I never disclose the real names of the homeless people I meet along the way. Although it might be okay, as it is not often that I ever see them twice. It is somewhat sad really. Chance encounters with people that are drifting through the streets, through life itself, do not usually show themselves to me twice. Years later, and further down the timeline of my life, I sometimes think I do see them again, meandering about on the hard streets of this city. It might be them. It might not.

The conversation was easy enough to start. It seemed as though she had much to say, almost as if she was just waiting for an opportunity to share it. What I noticed besides her crowded backpack and her faded lunch cooler was the red tips of her fingers. It meant only one thing, Flamin Hot Cheetos. "Nope," she tells me, "Flamin Hot Funyuns", and she smiles. Funny, I didn't even know there was such a snack chip. I ask her how in the world she could eat those on such a hot day. She points to her faded backpack and responds, "I have some water."

It was obvious to me by the way she was dressed, and the amount of stuff she had with her, that she was in fact more than likely homeless. You can tell. I sat down on a bench close to the one she was sitting on, and I propped my bike up on the edge of that bench. We talked about bikes, about grandkids and children. Debra tell me that she has 21 grandkids and 5 children. "WOW!" I exclaim, "That's a lot of grandbabies." She says the youngest is 3 years old, and then proceeds to share all about the others.

I ask her if she is staying at the shelter here in town. She tells me that she sleeps there most of the time, but last night she slept in the tents; the tents they set up along the river. "Tents?" I ask her. I had heard about tents along the river, I have just never seen any riding along. But then again, I don't guess I've ever really looked for them. So, we continue to talk Debra and I – about kids, grandkids, bikes, tents, Funyuns, and I finished a water bottle of my own, and get up to leave.

She said she's heard of a lady giving bikes away to homeless people, and that she might try to get herself one. I tell her that I hope she does and I do. After about 20 minutes,

I tell her I need to get on down the trail because I need to pick up my own grandson. She tells me she needs to head back downtown herself; lunch is at one o' clock. I get on my bike, and before I leave, I tell her I hope she gets her bike. She tells me she hopes so too and I ride off.

I was glad I met her today. It was so random, very much a chance encounter. She seemed so eager to share, seemed very content sitting along the river under the shade of the big tree, eating her chips, guarding her faded backpack and belongings. She did not share much else on this day. I would imagine that back when her world was spinning in the right direction, the conversation might have been different.

There was a time when it never registered in my mind, that all the desperate transient drifters, the empty-eyed people with the sun-scorched faces, used to be someone's bright-eyed child, somebody's mother, and as the case was today, someone's grandmother. It is a very sobering thought, one that fills me with sadness.

Now off the trails and my bike, I am cooling off in my vehicle, and my mind shifts to Debra's kids and her grandkids. I feel complete and utter sadness for this woman. I think of my own mother as I drive, and I did actually think of her as I was talking to Debra. Although at that time the thoughts were screaming out in my head, I did not let them turn into words. I just let them remain my own silent angry thoughts. How on earth does this happen? I think even now, I do not know all the details. I know only a fraction of Debra's story, but I cannot come up with one single horrible or atrocious act, which would cause me to let my own mother become a homeless drifter. I'm sorry I just can't.

Now home and in front of my laptop, I think about Debra. I wonder if she has made it back to the shelter. I wonder if she is sleeping in a tent. I look outside and notice that the dark skies are coming in quickly with the late hour. I wonder where she has chosen to lay her head down tonight. I find myself hoping that Debra does, in fact, get one of those free bikes they are giving away to the homeless.

WILLIAM'S JOURNEY

The dinner shift on this chilly October night began much like all the other ones began, with the exception of one thing; William was missing. I thought things seemed somewhat quiet. Something just wasn't right, and about an hour into the dinner shift, I realized what it was. When William is in the kitchen, everyone knows it. He has a presence uncharacteristic of the other men at the shelter. He is one of the homeless men that work alongside the volunteers. His childlike demeanor and ever-present smile light up the kitchen each Saturday.

Yesterday however, he was gone. At first, I thought that maybe he got out. If anyone deserved to make it out of the shelter, it is William. I believe that he is one of the few regulars that has hope. You can tell by the drive and determination in which he goes about his duties each evening. He deserves his own address. He deserves new beginnings. Unfortunately, he did not get out, not in the way I had hoped. William, after having a rough week with his regular meds, ended up in the psychiatric unit of St John's Hospital. I was told with any luck, he would be out by Christmas.

My hope for William is that he will stay strong in his mind. He is not like most grown men. On the inside, he seems like a young boy. When not busy, you will always see William walking around the kitchen with a plate of food in his hand. Chances are it will be loaded high with all the sugary sweets he can find and he knows just where to look. It seems to me that life had in fact, dealt William some rough blows. God only knows how he ended up homeless. Only God knows what happened along the way, to cause William to get to a point where he needed psychiatric meds in the first place. I would venture to bet that the life William is living now is not the life he had envisioned for himself.

This is what I do know; William has hope. You can see it; you can feel it. He is one of the guys that has in a very short amount of time, impacted my heart, and the hearts of the others I work with. I am not sure what people see when they look at William, hard to tell. There is an entire demographic of people, that look at the homeless in an entirely different light. And that light is not bright at all, but very negative and dark. When I look at William, I see a young man that is trying to hold on to some sense of normalcy, in a society that continually tells him, you are not normal. I see a man that is trying to become whole again. I see a man that has been dealt a hard life. Whether or not he was the dealer remains to be seen, but what I see clearest of all – is a man that matters.

Miriam Walker

ABOUT THE AUTHOR

Miriam Walker is freelance writer. Her work has appeared on many online platforms, and she is a weekly contributor to several fitness blogs. She attended The University of Nebraska, while continuing to write. She has four children and four grandchildren. She enjoys riding her bike in her free time, and resides in the Tulsa area. Miriam Walker continues to work with the homeless of her city, through her ministry. Homeless Has a Name is her first book.

If you'd like to contact Miriam Walker, please reach out via email at miriamwalkerbooks@gmail.com.

Made in the USA
Lexington, KY
17 November 2019

57202686R00061